First published in Great Britain 2016
by Search Press Limited
Wellwood, North Farm Road,
Tunbridge Wells, Kent TN2 3DR

© 2013 Kamilla Svanlund, Clara Falk, Ewa Andinsson och Andina Förlag &
Produktion AB
Original title: Vantar för alla årstider
First published by Andina Förlag & Produktion AB, Sweden

English Translation by Burravoe Translation Services

© Andina Förlag
© Text and knitting patterns: Clara Falk and Kamilla Svanlund
Technical illustrations: Kamilla Svanlund
© Photography: Ewa Andinsson
Graphic design: Sofia Brolin, Brolin form & kommunikation AB
Repro: Elanders
Print: Elanders, Hungary

ISBN: 978-1-78221-320-8

If you have difficulty in obtaining any of the materials and equipment
mentioned in this book, then please visit the Search Press website for details
of suppliers: www.searchpress.com

Printed in China

Clara Falk | Kamilla Svanlund

PRETTY KNITTED HANDS

MITTENS & WRIST WARMERS FOR ALL SEASONS

Search Press

CONTENTS

SPRING/SUMMER

AUTUMN

FOREWORD

We have been friends for many years, following each other's lives and knitting – all thanks to the internet. We came to know each other because we each have a blog where we write about our knitting and designing, and also sell patterns. After years of knowing each other online, we finally met face-to-face over a cup of coffee when Kamilla was on holiday in Gothenburg, where Clara lives. We immediately started planning a book about our favourite knitting projects – mittens!

Why mittens? Because they are so fantastically versatile! They keep your hands warm, of course, but they are also beautiful and a great way to accessorise any outfit.

We like to make mittens for all seasons – mittens that do the job when you are out for a walk in the cool early days of spring in a thin jacket; mittens for icy winter mornings when you are on your way to work; and beautiful wrist warmers that you could wear for picking summer flowers. The wools range from the sheerest silk and cool linen through to wonderfully warm wool.

Mittens are also great for trying out new techniques. If you want to learn how to knit cables or to knit using several colours, but don't want to knit a whole jumper, mittens are an ideal place to start!

Clara & Kamilla

TECHNIQUES

DOUBLE-POINTED NEEDLES OR A MAGIC LOOP?

Whether you use a magic loop or double-pointed needles is a matter of taste, as the end results are the same; it is just the process that differs. Kamilla prefers to use double-pointed needles while Clara prefers a magic loop. We suggest you try both and then choose the one you like best.

DOUBLE-POINTED NEEDLES

In Sweden we normally use five needles when using double-pointed needles: four to hold the stitches and a fifth to knit with.
We call the needles that hold the stitches 1, 2, 3 and 4. Needle 1 is where the row starts and 4 is where the row finishes.
It is important to remember not to twist the cast-on stitches as you knit the first row. If you lay down the knitting, the cast-on edge should point inwards.

THE MAGIC LOOP

The magic loop is a technique that enables you to make even small knitted items on a circular needle. The needle needs to be as long and flexible as possible; we recommend at least 80cm (31½in).
To use this technique, you divide your work in two, with half the stitches on one needle and half on the other. Place the needles parallel with each other. Draw the rear needle out so that the stitches slip back onto the cable until you have a small loop on the left-hand side. Your right-hand needle is now free to start knitting. When the stitches on the left needle have been knitted, you turn the knitting and again draw the cable out so that the stitches that have not yet been knitted are on the front needle. There are good videos on YouTube giving more detailed instructions – just search for Magic Loop.

Long tail cast-on

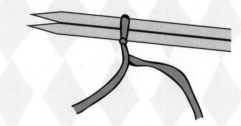

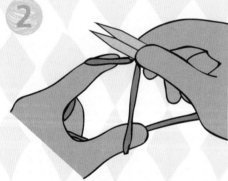

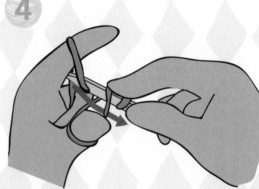

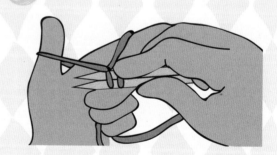

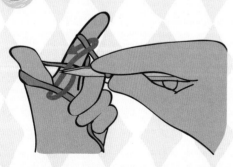

CASTING ON

LONG TAIL CAST-ON

Both of us mainly use long tail cast-on (see diagrams opposite) when we knit mittens, and all the mittens in this book use this method unless otherwise specified.

It is the 'classic' Swedish cast-on, and the one most often taught in schools. It is well suited to mittens because it gives just the right amount of elasticity. Method: take a long length of yarn and make a loop with a slip knot, and place the loop on two needles (see diagram 1). Hold the yarn from the long tail over the thumb and the ball end over the forefinger of your left hand as in diagram 2. Take the needles under, over and under the yarn as shown in diagram 3 and then draw the needles through the loop formed at the thumb (diagram 4). Pull firm and repeat from diagram 2–5 until you have the required number of stitches.

CABLE CAST-ON

The cable cast-on method is an excellent choice when you need to cast on stitches in the middle of a piece of knitting, as you only use one strand of yarn.

Make a loop with a slip knot and place it on your left needle. Increase it to two stitches by knitting into the front and back of the stitch (for the Martha mitten, see page 82, you can leave out these stages as you will have existing

stitches to work from). Insert the needle between the stitches, pass the yarn around the needle and draw a loop through. Place this new stitch on the left needle. Insert the needle between the two top stitches and repeat until you have the required number of stitches.

PROVISIONAL CAST-ON

There are several ways of doing a provisional cast-on. The one we have used is based on a long tail cast-on.

Make a slip knot with two strands of yarn. One is the yarn you will knit with, and the other should be in a contrasting colour because you will take it out later.

Hold the contrasting yarn over your thumb and the yarn you will be knitting with over your forefinger. Cast on as many stitches as you need according to your pattern (don't count the slip knot), then remove the slip knot and start knitting according to the pattern.

When you have finished and are ready to pick up these stitches again, you remove the contrasting yarn and will now have open stitches to pick up on to the needle again.

I-CORD CAST-ON

Cast on 3 stitches.

Row 1: Knit the 3 stitches, then slip all 3 back to the left needle.

Row 2: Knit the first stitch front and back (creating 2 stitches), knit to the end, then slip the last 3 stitches back to the left needle.

Repeat Row 2 until you have the required number of stitches.

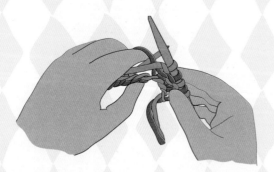

OTHER TECHNIQUES

LATVIAN BRAID

Cast on the number of stitches you need according to the pattern using the colours stated. Choose one colour to be A and another to be B.

Row 1: *K1 with A, k1 with B*, repeat from * to * to end of row.

Row 2: *P1 with A, p1 with B*, repeat from * to * to end of row. Each time, pass the new yarn **over** the yarn you have just knitted with.

Row 3: *P1 with A, p1 with B*, repeat from * to * to end of row. Each time, pass the new yarn **under** the yarn you have just knitted with.

I-CORD

Cast on 3 stitches with double-pointed needles using a provisional cast-on. Knit the 3 stitches, but do not turn your work. Push the stitches to the other end of the needle and knit the row again. The yarn will run behind the knitting at the start of the row, and this makes a little tube form, which is the i-cord.

Continue until you have knitted the desired number of rows. Put the 3 stitches onto a piece of scrap yarn and then knit according to the pattern. Sew together the 3 first and last stitches using Kitchener stitch, or grafting, when the mitten is finished (see page 14).

STITCH MARKERS

Stitch markers are very useful! You can use a paper clip, a piece of yarn or pretty, purpose-made markers. Whichever you choose, it is a good idea to mark where you need to create a cable or a thumb gusset, as it is easy to miss the spot.

SLIP, SLIP, KNIT (SSK)
– a decrease that slants to the left
With your right needle, slip next 2 stitches as if you were going to knit them, move these stitches back to the left needle and knit both stitches through the back.

KNIT 2 STITCHES TOGETHER (K2TOG)
– a decrease that slants to the right
Knit two stitches together.

INCREASE 2 (INC 2)
– a centred increase
Knit 1, but leave the stitch on the left needle. Knit into the rear of the same stitch then knit into the front of it.

SL1, K2TOG, PSSO
– a centred decrease
Slip a stitch as if you were going to purl it, knit the next two stitches together and pass the slipped stitch over the two stitches you have knitted together.

INCREASE RIGHT AND LEFT
Increase slanting to the left (m1l):
Pick up the yarn between the stitches with the left needle as shown in the diagram (i.e. from the front). If there are several strands, use the colour that the increased stitch needs to be in. Knit the stitch you have picked up through the back loop.
Increase slanting to the right (m1r):
Pick up the yarn between the stitches with the left needle as shown in the diagram (i.e. from the back). If there are several strands, use the colour that the increased stitch needs to be in. Knit the stitch you have picked up through the front loop.

Increase left

Increase right

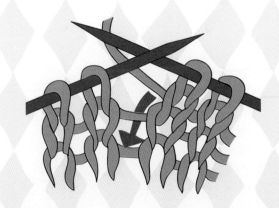

13

CASTING OFF

The cast-off we have used most in this book is a normal cast-off, which is not very stretchy, so you should be careful how tightly you knit these stitches.

The cast-off is worked as follows: work a stitch the same way as the stitch below it (knit over knit, purl over purl); work the next stitch as the stitch below. Now take the first stitch you worked and slip it over the most recent stitch. You have now cast off a stitch. Work a new stitch, and pull the last stitch over the new stitch. Continue in this way until you have cast off the required number of stitches. When you have cast off all the stitches in the row, break off the yarn, thread it through the last stitch and draw tight.

I-CORD CAST-OFF

Start by casting on three stitches using a provisional cast-on. Knit the first two stitches, then knit the next two stitches together through the back of the stitches. Transfer the knitted stitches back onto the left needle.

Now knit as follows: *K2, k2tog through the back of the stitches, transfer these back to the left needle. Repeat from * until there are no more stitches. You will now have 3 sts left on the needle. Pick up the provisional cast-on and sew the i-cord together using Kitchener stitch, or grafting.

KITCHENER STITCH (GRAFTING)

Divide the stitches you have left between two needles. Break off the yarn to a length of 20cm (7¾in) and thread the yarn through a tapestry needle.

Method for Kitchener stitch:

1. Insert the tapestry needle as if you were going to purl the first stitch on the front knitting needle (the needle closest to you), draw the yarn through the stitch but leave the stitch on the needle.
2. Insert the tapestry needle as if you were going to knit the first stitch on the rear needle, draw the yarn though but leave the stitch on the needle and tighten it a little.
3. Insert the tapestry needle as if you were going to knit the first stitch on the front needle, and release the stitch from the needle.
4. Insert the tapestry needle as if you were going to purl a stitch on the front needle, draw the stitch through but leave it on the needle.
5. Insert the tapestry needle as if you were going to purl the first stitch on the rear needle, and release the stitch from the needle.
6. Insert the tapestry needle as if you were going to knit a stitch on the rear needle, draw the stitch through but leave it on the needle.

Repeat steps 3–6 until you have two stitches left. Repeat steps 3 and 5 only on these two stitches. Draw the yarn though to the purl side and fasten off.

ALTERNATIVE YARNS

If you cannot source the yarns stated in the patterns, you can use yarn of a similar weight and yardage to make the mittens and wrist warmers in this book.

Abbreviations

k – knit
ktbl – twisted knit stitch (knit through back of loop)
k2tog – knit two stitches together
inc2 – increase 2
m1l – make 1 left (increase one left-slanting stitch)
m1r – make 1 right (increase one right-slanting stitch)
p – purl

p2tog – purl 2 stitches together
pm – place a new marker on the needle
psso – pass the slipped stitch over the knitted stitch(es)
sl1 – slip 1
sm – slip marker
ssk – slip, slip, knit
st(s) – stitch(es)
YO – yarn over

Insert the needle purlwise

 TIP!

BLOCKING
When you have knitted your mittens they may be a bit bobbly if you have used several colours. You can smooth out your finished work by wetting it and leaving it to dry. Do this either by pinning down the mittens and dampening them with a spray bottle or by soaking them under a running tap and gently stretching them out.

Insert the needle knitwise

ABOUT THE CHARTS
The charts should be read from bottom to top, and from right to left, unless otherwise stated.

SPRING/
SUMMER

HETTY

Cool bamboo wrist warmers
in mesh pattern

SIZE
Circumference: 15cm (6in)
Total length: 23cm (9in)
Length of thumb gusset: 7cm (2¾in)
From end of thumb gusset to cast-off of wrist warmer: 3.5cm (1½in)

MATERIALS
Needles: 3mm (UK 11, US 3)
Yarn: Sirdar Baby Bamboo
96m/104yds/50g, 80% bamboo, 20% wool
2 balls: 122 Groovy Green

TENSION/GAUGE
26 sts x 32 rows = 10 x 10cm (4 x 4in) in textured knit

INSTRUCTIONS
Cast on 40 sts and knit 6 rows of twisted rib: *K1 into back of stitch, p1*, repeat from * to * to end.
Row 7: K2tog, k1, *YO, slip 1, k2, psso*, repeat from * to * until 1 st remains, k1.
Row 8 and all even rows: K.
Row 9: K1, *YO, slip 1, k2, psso*, repeat from * to * until 2 sts remain, k2tog.
Row 11: *YO, slip 1, k2, psso*, repeat from * to * to end of row.
Row 13: YO, k2tog, *YO, slip 1, k2, psso*, repeat until 1 st remains, k1.
Repeat Rows 9–13 for 19 rows. Whether you are using circular needles or double-pointed needles, you will need to move stitches between the needles (although not at the beginning or end of the row) to make the pattern work. After 19 rows of the pattern, start the increases for the thumb gusset. Put a marker before the last two stitches on a row that has been knitted as a Row 9. Increase on both sides of the second to last stitch by picking up the yarn between the stitches and knitting through the back loop. Knit into the back of the stitches between the markers. Continue working in pattern for other stitches.

When you have 17 sts in the thumb gusset, place them on a piece of scrap yarn. Cast on 3 sts and continue to work in pattern for another 7 rows. Knit 6 rows of twisted rib and cast off in rib.

THUMB
Put the 17 sts from the scrap yarn back onto the needles. Pick up 3 sts around thumb hole (20 sts on needles) and knit 5 rows of twisted knit stitches (ktbl). Cast off.

FINISHING
Fasten off all ends and block the wrist warmers.

SIGRID

Romantic, summery wrist warmers in linen

SIZE
Circumference: 21cm (8¼in) at widest point, 13cm (5in) at narrowest
Length of thumb gusset: 7cm (2¾in)
From end of thumb gusset to end of wrist warmer: 5cm (2in)

MATERIALS
Needles: 3mm (UK 11, US 3)
Crochet hook: 0.6mm (UK 6, US 14)
Yarn: Karin Öberg Kalinka Lingarn 320m/350yds/100g, 100% linen
1 skein: Himmel
Beads: approx. 50, size 7/0

TENSION/GAUGE
22 sts x 28 rows = 10 x 10cm (4 x 4in) in stocking stitch (US stockinette stitch)

CROCHETING IN THE BEADS
Thread the bead onto the crochet hook and insert the crochet hook into the front of the stitch as if you were going to purl it. Draw the stitch through the bead and place the stitch back onto the left needle.

INSTRUCTIONS
Cast on 40 sts and work in rib for 8 rows: *K2, p2*, repeat from * to * to end. Knit one row.
Row 10: K8, k2tog, YO, k1, YO, ssk, k27.
Row 11. K.
Repeat these two rows. At every 4th row, crochet a bead into the stitch between the YOs.
Start decreases 2.5cm (1in) from the end of the ribbing: K29, k2tog, pm, ssk, k7.
The decrease row is repeated five times, every 8th row. Knit the pattern in parallel with the decreases.

THUMB GUSSET
Start the thumb gusset 61 rows (about 19cm/7½in) from the end of the ribbing. This is knitted 7 sts from the stitch between the YOs, which means increases on both sides of the first stitch on the left wrist warmer and the 22nd stitch on the right wrist warmer. Place a marker each side of the stitch and increase inside the markers.
Increase as follows: pick up a stitch on either side of stitch 1 and 22 respectively by lifting up the horizontal piece of yarn between two stitches and knitting through the back loop. Repeat five times, every 4th row. You will now have 13 sts between the markers.
Work another row and then put the 13 sts onto a piece of scrap yarn. Increase 1 st and continue to work in pattern. Work another 9 rows (make sure you finish with a Row 10). Then work 7 rows of ribbing and cast off in rib.

THUMB
Put the 13 sts from the scrap yarn back onto the needles. Pick up 3 sts around thumb hole (20 sts on needles). *K2, p2*, repeat from * to * to end of row for 4 rows. Cast off.

FINISHING
Fasten off all ends and block the wrist warmers.

BARBARA

Dainty wrist warmers with i-cords

SIZE
Circumference: 22cm (8¾in) at widest point, 16cm (6¼in) at narrowest
Total length: 17cm (6¾in)
Length of thumb gusset: 4cm (1½in)
From end of thumb gusset to end of wrist warmer: 5cm (2in)

MATERIALS
Needles: 2.5mm (UK 12, US 2)
Yarn: Teetee Elegant
500m/547yds/50g, 70% worsted wool, 30% tussah silk
1 skein in colour A: 101 Orange
1 skein in colour B: 100 Yellow

TENSION/GAUGE
19 rows x 17 sts = 5 x 5cm (2 x 2in) in stocking stitch (US stockinette stitch)

These wrist warmers are both knitted the same way – it does not matter which is right or left.

INSTRUCTIONS

Cast on 4 sts in colour A with a provisional cast-on and knit these as an i-cord for 56 rows (see pages 11 and 12). Break off the yarn and put the stitches aside on a piece of yarn in a different colour.

Using colour B, pick up 56 sts along the i-cord, and then begin working Chart 1 (see opposite). Repeat the pattern ten times each row.

When you have finished Chart 1, break off the colour B yarn and cast on 4 sts with a provisional cast-on in colour A. Transfer these back to the left needle, and then cast off with an i-cord cast-off in colour A. When you have four stitches left on the needle, transfer these over to a different coloured piece of yarn. Break off the colour A yarn and pick up 56 sts with colour B on top of the i-cord that was created when casting off. Now work 10 rows in colour B. Next comes the thumb gusset, which you make between needles 1 and 4 as follows:

Row 1: K1, YO, k to end of row, YO.
Row 2: K.

Repeat these two rows six times; this will increase the total number of stitches by 12.

Break off the yarn, and then set aside the first 7 sts from needle 1 and the last 6 sts from needle 4 on a stitch holder or on a different coloured piece of yarn.

Cast on a new stitch, which will now be the first stitch on needle 1, and knit for 20 rows.

Break off the colour B yarn, and cast on 4 sts in colour A using a provisional cast-on. Then cast off in colour A using an i-cord cast-off. When you have 4 sts left on the needle, transfer them to a different coloured piece of yarn.

THUMB

Pick up the 13 sts you set aside for the thumb gusset and pick up 5 sts around the thumb hole with colour B (18 sts on needles). Knit 10 rows and cast off in colour A using an i-cord cast-off in the same way as you have cast off the rest of the wrist warmer.

FINISHING

Sew all the i-cords together using Kitchener stitch (see page 14), fasten off all ends and block the wrist warmers.

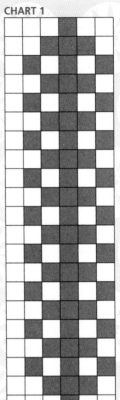

CHART 1

☐ colour A

■ colour B

OLGA

Bavarian cable wrist warmers

SIZE
Circumference (without thumb gusset):
14–20cm (5½–7¾in); the cables make the
wrist warmer stretchy
Length of thumb gusset: 8cm (3¼in)
From thumb to decrease: 3cm (1¼in)

MATERIALS
Needles: 3mm (UK 11, US 3)
Yarn: Debbie Bliss Baby Cashmerino
125m/136yds/50g, 55% merino wool,
33% acrylic, 12% cashmere
2 balls: 02 Apple

TENSION/GAUGE
24 sts x 18 rows = 10 x 10cm (4 x 4in) in
stocking stitch (US stockinette stitch)

INSTRUCTIONS
RIGHT WRIST WARMER
Cast on 50 sts. Work 7 rows twisted rib: *K1tbl,
p1*, repeat from * to * to end. Now see Chart 1
(opposite) for the first cable.
Work Chart 1 until you have knitted 35 rows. Begin
the increase for the thumb gusset: the gusset is
worked in twisted knit stitches (ktbl). Knit 10 sts as
per Chart 1. Increase by picking up a stitch on each
side of the knit stitch. Place stitch markers each side
of the picked-up stitches to mark the gusset.
Increase every 3rd row until the gusset has 17
stitches, continuing to work the other stitches as
per Chart 1.
Place the 17 sts for the gusset on a piece of scrap
yarn and cast on a stitch above the gusset. Work
Chart 1 for a further 7 rows.

CAST OFF
K1tbl, p1, slip the knit stitch over the purl stitch,
repeat from * to *.

THUMB
Put the 17 sts from the scrap of yarn back on the
needles. Pick up 3 sts around the thumb hole. You
will now have 20 sts on the needles. Work 4 rows
of twisted knit stitches (ktbl). Cast off.

LEFT WRIST WARMER
Work as right wrist warmer, but use Chart 2 (see
opposite) instead of Chart 1.

FINISHING
Fasten off all ends and block the wrist warmers.

ROW 1, CHART 1

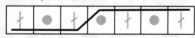

Transfer 4 sts to a cable needle, keep
behind the work, work 3 sts (k1tbl, p1,
k1tbl), then work the 4 sts from the
cable needle (p1, k1tbl, p1, k1tbl)

ROW 1, CHART 2

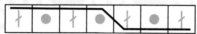

Transfer 3 sts to a cable needle, keep in
front of the work, work 4 sts (k1tbl, p1,
k1tbl, p1), then work the 3 sts on the
cable needle (k1tbl, p1, k1tbl)

CHART 1

●	↓	●	↓	●	↓	●	↓	●	↓	8
●	↓	●	↓	●	↓	●	↓	●	↓	7
●	↓	●	↓	●	↓	●	↓	●	↓	6
●	↓	●	↓	●	↓	●	↓	●	↓	5
●	↓	●	↓	●	↓	●	↓	●	↓	4
●	↓	●	↓	●	↓	●	↓	●	↓	3
●	↓	●	↓	●	↓	●	↓	●	↓	2
●	↓	↓	●	↓	●	↓	●	↓	↓	1

CHART 2

●	↓	●	↓	●	↓	●	↓	●	↓	8
●	↓	●	↓	●	↓	●	↓	●	↓	7
●	↓	●	↓	●	↓	●	↓	●	↓	6
●	↓	●	↓	●	↓	●	↓	●	↓	5
●	↓	●	↓	●	↓	●	↓	●	↓	4
●	↓	●	↓	●	↓	●	↓	●	↓	3
●	↓	●	↓	●	↓	●	↓	●	↓	2
●	↓	↓	●	↓	↓	●	↓	●	↓	1

● = p

↓ = twisted knit stitch (ktbl)

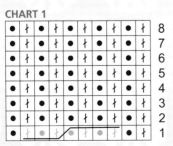

ELSA
Wrist warmers with leaves

SIZE
Circumference: 14cm (5½in)
Total length: 17cm (6¾in)
Length of thumb gusset: 4cm (1½in)
From end of gusset to end of wrist warmer:
5cm (2in)

MATERIALS
Needles: 2.5mm (UK 12, US 2)
Yarn: Malabrigo Lace
430m/470yds/50g, 100% merino wool
1 skein: 037 Lettuce

TENSION/GAUGE
19 rows x 17 sts = 5 x 5cm (2 x 2in) in
stocking stitch (US stockinette stitch)

These wrist warmers are both knitted the same way – it does not matter which is right or left.

INSTRUCTIONS
Cast on 56 sts. Then knit broken moss stitch as follows:
Rows 1 and 3: K.
Row 2: *K1, p1*, repeat from * to * to end of row.
Row 4: *P1, K1*, repeat from * to * to end of row.
Repeat these 4 rows five times to produce broken moss stitch.
Then work Chart 1 (see page 28); Chart 1 shows the stitches that belong to one needle. The chart is repeated four times per row. When you have knitted Rows 1–26, start the thumb gusset.
Work Chart 2 (see page 29) on needle 1, and continue to work Chart 1 (Rows 11–26) on the remaining needles.
Once you have finished this chart, put the last 20 stitches from needle 1 onto a stitch holder and cast on 4 new stitches behind the gusset. Now work Rows 11–34 of Chart 1. Work 4 rows of broken moss stitch twice (8 rows).
Cast off loosely knitwise.

THUMB
Pick up the 20 sts you set aside earlier and pick up 4 sts around the thumb hole. You will now have 24 sts on the needles. Work purl on purl and knit on knit; the new stitches should be purled.
Work in this way for 5 rows. Work 4 rows of broken moss stitch twice (8 rows).
Cast off loosely knitwise.

FINISHING
Fasten off all ends and block the wrist warmers.

CHART 1

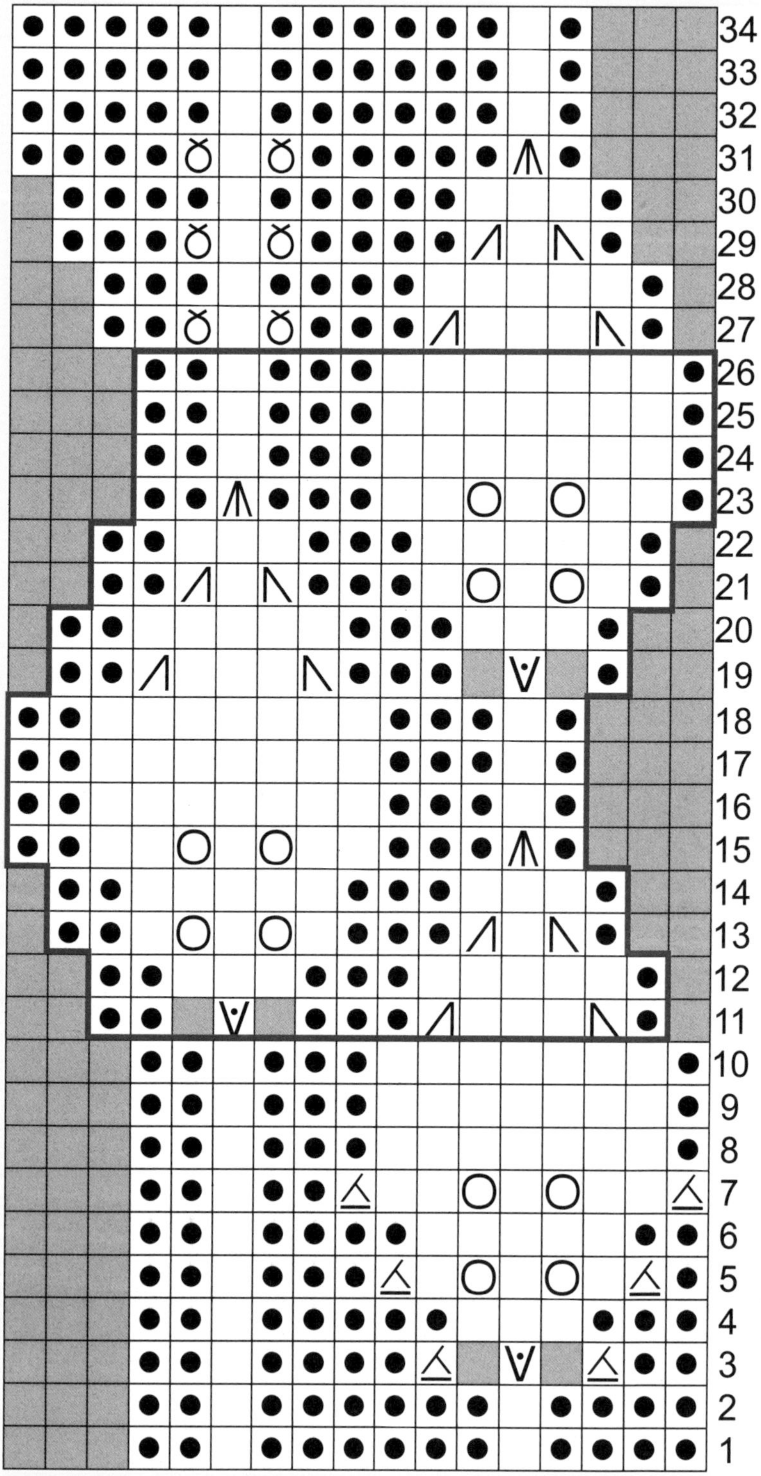
34
33
32
31
30
29
28
27
26
25
24
23
22
21
20
19
18
17
16
15
14
13
12
11
10
9
8
7
6
5
4
3
2
1

ELSA

☐ k
● p
╱ k2tog
╲ ssk
ŏ m1
○ YO
⋀ sl1, k2tog, psso
v inc2
⟋ p2tog
☐ repeat
▨ no stitch

CHART 2

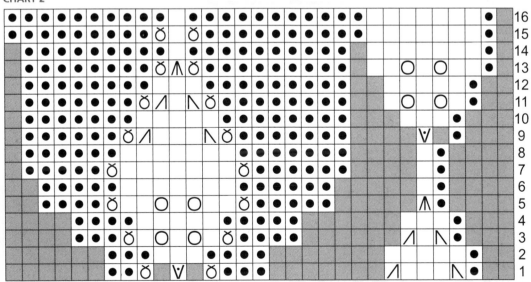

ELISABETH

Wedding wrist warmers in silk

SIZE
Circumference: Approx. 16cm (6¼in) at narrowest point
Total length: 28cm (11in)
Length of thumb gusset: 7cm (2¾in)
From end of gusset to end of wrist warmers: 4.5cm (1¾in)

MATERIALS
Needles: 2.5mm (UK 12, US 2)
Yarn: BC Garn Jaipur Silk Fino 600m/656yds/100g,100% silk
1 skein: H49 Natural

TENSION/GAUGE
19 rows x 17 sts = 5 x 5cm (2 x 2in) in stocking stitch (US stockinette stitch)

INSTRUCTIONS

Cast on 3 sts and work as per Chart 1 (see page 32), starting at Row 1. Work this part by turning. When you get to Row 37 in the chart, divide the knitting across 4 double-pointed needles and knit round until you reach Row 49.

After Row 49, repeat Rows 50–51 ten times. Continue by repeating these rows, knitting the thumb gusset at the same time.

THUMB GUSSET: RIGHT WRIST WARMER

After 34 sts: Pm, k1, pm; the increases should be worked inside these markers.

Row 1: Work up to the first marker, sm, m1r, k to marker, m1l, sm, work remaining stitches as per established pattern.

Rows 2–3: K.

Repeat these 3 rows seven times. You will now have 15 sts between the markers. Set these aside on a piece of yarn and cast on a new stitch in the thumb hole on the next row.

THUMB GUSSET: LEFT WRIST WARMER

This is worked the same way as the right wrist warmer but the markers are placed after 9 sts.

When you have knitted the gusset, continue to repeat Rows 50–51 four times.

Work Rows 52–57 of the chart, then knit twisted ribbing: *K1tbl, p1*, repeat from * to * to end of row for 5 rows.

Cast off in rib.

THUMB

Pick up the 15 sts you set aside for the thumb gusset and pick up 7 sts in the thumb hole. You will now have a total of 22 sts. Knit twisted ribbing: *K1tbl, p1* for 5 rows.

Cast off in rib.

FINISHING

Fasten off all ends and block the wrist warmers.

CHART 1

	k		k2tog		m1		sl1, k2tog, psso
●	p		ssk	○	YO		no stitch

ELISABETH

LOTTIE

Wrist warmers with
candy stripes

SIZE
Circumference: 16cm (6¼in) excluding
thumb gusset
Total length: 20cm (7¾in)
Length of thumb gusset: 6.5cm (2½in)
*From end of gusset to cast-off of wrist
warmer:* 3cm (1¼in)

MATERIALS
Needles: 3mm (UK 11, US 3)
Yarn: Sirdar Baby Bamboo
95m/104yds/50g, 80% bamboo,
20% wool
1 ball in colour A: 173 Red
1 ball in colour B: 131 Cream

TENSION/GAUGE
31 sts x 32 rows = 10 x 10cm (4 x 4in) in
coloured knitting

INSTRUCTIONS
Cast on 48 sts in colour A and knit 4 rows of twisted
rib: *K1tbl, p1*, repeat from * to * to end of row.
Continue by following Row 5 from the bottom of Chart
1 (see page 36). In Row 5, decrease one stitch by k2tog
at the start of the row. You will now have 47 sts. Work
up to the green marker for the thumb gusset.
Now work Chart 2 (see page 37) in for thumb gusset
with Chart 1. Place stitch markers in the pattern so that
it is easier to see where Chart 2 sits.
When you have finished Chart 2, you will have 13 sts
between the markers. Place these 13 sts on a piece of
scrap yarn. Cast on 3 new stitches behind the gusset
and continue to work Chart 1.
Cast off in rib.

THUMB
Put the 13 sts from the piece of scrap yarn back on the
needles. Pick up a further 7 sts in the thumb hole. You
will now have 20 sts on the needles. Knit the thumb as
per Chart 3 (see page 37).
Cast off in rib.

FINISHING
Fasten off all ends and block the wrist warmers.

CHART 1

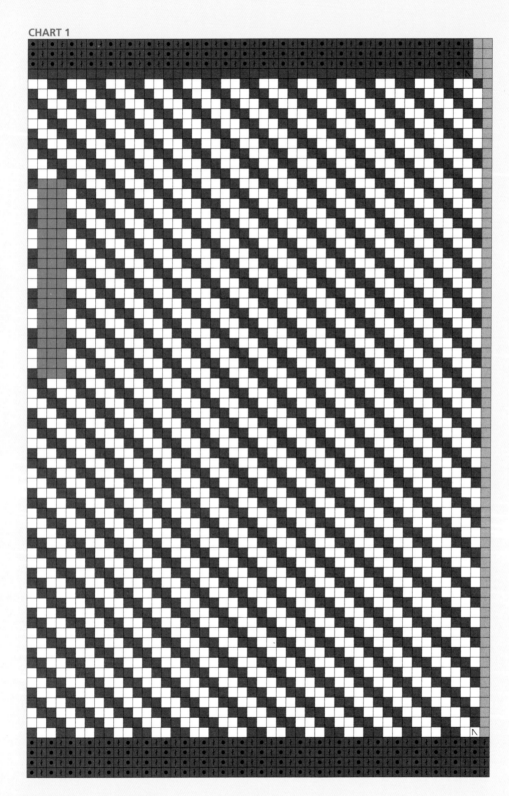

CHART 2

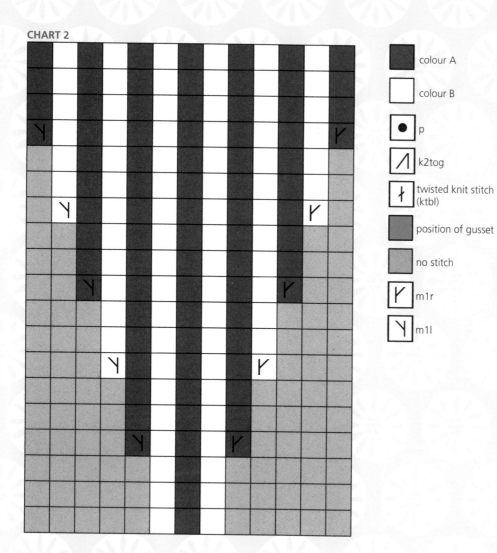

■	colour A
□	colour B
●	p
⁄	k2tog
⼁	twisted knit stitch (ktbl)
■	position of gusset
■	no stitch
Ƴ	m1r
Y	m1l

CHART 3

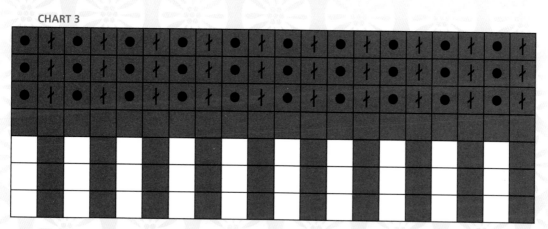

RITA

Cable wrist warmers

SIZE
Circumference: 16cm (6¼in)
Total length: 20cm (7¾in)
Length of thumb gusset: 5cm (2in)
From end of gusset to end of wrist warmer: 5cm (2in)

MATERIALS
Needles: 2.5mm (UK 12, US 2)
Yarn: Sandnes Garn Lanett Babyull
175m/191yds/50g, 100% merino
1 ball: 2317 Yellow

TENSION/GAUGE
17 sts x 18 rows = 5 x 5cm (2 x 2in) in cable pattern

These wrist warmers are both knitted the same way – it does not matter which is right or left.

INSTRUCTIONS
Cast on 102 sts and begin working Chart 1 (see page 40). The pattern within the red section should be repeated throughout the whole project, i.e. the first 6 stitches in the chart are only worked over the first 6 stitches of the row.

When you have finished Chart 1, move on to Chart 2 (see page 40). The first 4 rows in the chart are knitted only once at the start of the wrist warmer; the last 4 rows of the chart are knitted at the end of the wrist warmer. It is the rows between these rows that are repeated, and here too you repeat the stitches that are within the red section. The stitches before and after this section are the first and last stitches of the row. Place markers to make these easier to see.

When you have repeated Rows 5–16 twice, knit the thumb gusset alongside Chart 2. K1, pm, pick up the yarn between the stitches and knit through the back loop, pm and continue as per Chart 2.

Row 1: K the thumb gusset stitches and work the rest of the stitches as per chart.
Row 2: K1, sm, m1r, k to marker, m1l, sm, work remaining stitches as per chart.

Repeat these 2 rows seven times; you will now have 15 sts between the markers.

Knit 5 rows in which you k the thumb gusset stitches and the remaining stitches as per the chart. Set the thumb stitches aside and continue to work Chart 2.

When you have repeated Chart 2 five times, work the last 4 rows of the chart.

Cast off knit on knit and purl on purl.

THUMB
Pick up the 15 sts you set aside earlier and pick up 3 sts around thumb hole; you will now have 18 sts.
Work Chart 3 (see page 41).
Cast off knit on knit and purl on purl.

FINISHING
Fasten off all ends and block the wrist warmers.

CHART 1

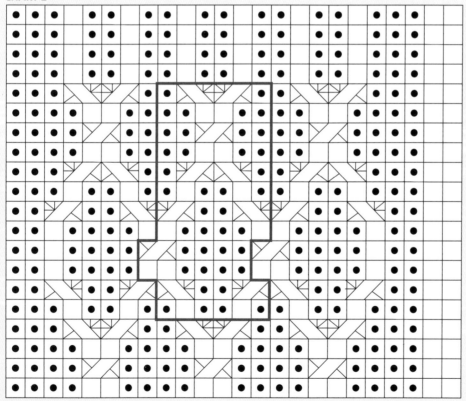

CHART 2

	k		ssk
•	p		repeat
/	k2tog		no stitch

Transfer 1 st to the cable needle, keep behind the work, k1, p the stitch on the cable needle

Transfer 1 st to the cable needle, keep in front of the work, p1, k the stitch on the cable needle

Transfer 1 st to the cable needle, keep in front of the work, p1, k the stitch on the cable needle

CHART 3

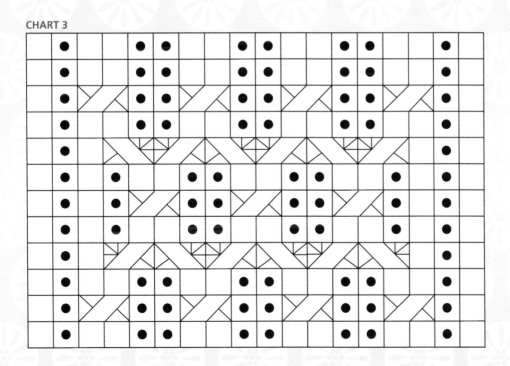

RITA

41

AUTUMN

STELLA

Wrist warmers with a
variation on raised cable

SIZE
Circumference: 19cm (7½in) measured at the
wrist without thumb gusset, though these are
very elastic
Total length: 22cm (8¾in)
Length of thumb gusset: 7cm (2¾in)
From end of gusset to cast-off of wrist warmer:
3cm (1¼in)

MATERIALS
Needles: 3.5mm (UK 9/10, US 4)
Yarn: Sublime Baby Cashmere Merino Silk
DK 116m/126yds/50g, 75% merino, 20% silk,
5% cashmere
2 balls: 219 Carrots

TENSION/GAUGE
22 sts x 28 rows = 10 x 10cm (4 x 4in) in
stocking stitch (US stockinette stitch)

INSTRUCTIONS
Cast on 48 sts.

RIGHT WRIST WARMER
Work Chart 1, Chart 2 (see page 46 for both
charts), *p2, k2*, repeat from * to * to end of
row for 46 rows. You will have knitted Charts
1 and 2 twice plus another 10 rows. Now work
Chart 3 (see page 46) over the last 4 sts in Chart 2,
while continuing to work the other stitches as per
pattern. Placing markers will help you see where
Chart 3 sits.
When you have completed Chart 3, you will have
16 sts between the markers. Place these on a piece
of scrap yarn. Cast on 2 sts and continue knitting
as per pattern. You are no longer knitting the cable
at the end of Chart 2; the new stitches are knitted
in rib.
Complete Charts 1 and 2 and cast off knit in knit
and purl in purl.

LEFT WRIST WARMER
Work Chart 1, *p2, k2* six times, Chart 2, *p2,
k2* ten times for 46 rows; you will have knitted
Charts 1 and 2 twice plus a further 10 rows.

Now work Chart 3 over the last 4 sts in Chart 2,
while continuing to work the other stitches as per
pattern. Placing markers will help you see where
Chart 3 should be.
When you have completed Chart 3, you will have
16 sts between the markers. Place these 16 sts on
a piece of scrap yarn. Cast on 2 sts and continue
knitting as per pattern. You are no longer knitting
the cable at the end of Chart 2; the new stitches
are knitted in rib.
Complete Charts 1 and 2 and cast off knit in knit
and purl in purl.

THUMB
Pick up 4 sts around the thumb hole and the 16 sts
you set aside earlier (20 sts on the needles), knit 4
rows and cast off.

FINISHING
Fasten off all ends and block the wrist warmers.

CHART 1

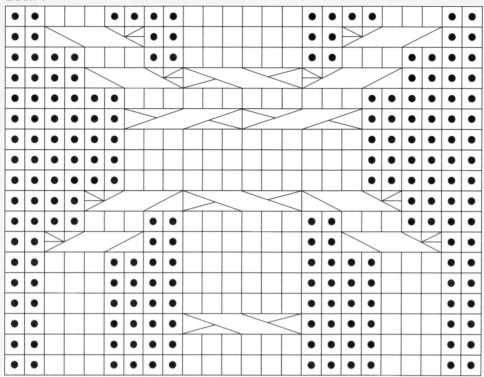

CHART 2

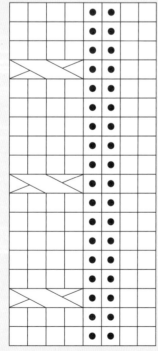

CHART 3

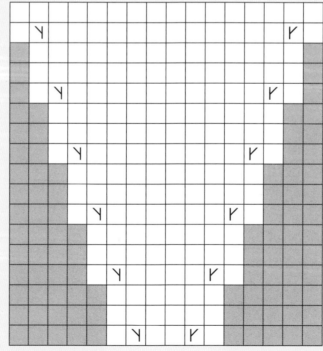

STELLA

 p    k

m1r   m1l

Transfer 2 sts to the cable needle,
keep behind the work, k2, k the
stitches on the cable needle

Transfer 3 sts to the cable needle,
keep in front of the work, p2, k the
stitches on the cable needle

Transfer 2 sts to the cable needle,
keep behind the work, k3, p the
stitches on the cable needle

Transfer 3 sts to the cable needle,
keep in front of the work, k3, p the
stitches on the cable needle

Transfer 3 sts to the cable needle,
keep behind the work, k3, p the
stitches on the cable needle

SIZE

Circumference: 10cm (4in) at widest point and 7.8cm (3in) at narrowest
Total length: 27cm (10¾in)
Length of thumb gusset: 10cm (4in)
From end of gusset to end of wrist warmer: 5.5cm (2¼in)
The cables make these wrist warmers very stretchy

MATERIALS

Needles: 4mm (UK 8, US 6)
Yarn: Drops Nepal
75m/82yds/50g, 65% wool, 35% alpaca
2 skeins: 0100 Off-white

TENSION/GAUGE

9 sts x 14 rows = 5 x 5cm (2 x 2in) in stocking stitch (US stockinette stitch)

RACHEL

Wrist warmers with chunky cables

INSTRUCTIONS

Cast on 40 sts.

Work ribbing: *K2, p2*, repeat from * to * to end of row.

Work 10 rows of ribbing and then work the first 22 sts as per Chart 1 (see page 50); this is the upper side of the wrist warmers. The remaining 18 sts are the inside and you continue to work these knit on knit and purl on purl.

When you reach Row 27 of the chart, start the thumb gusset. When you have finished the chart, begin the chart once more; the 22 sts on the upper side must always be worked as per the chart on the upper side of the hand, you knit the inside as follows:

THUMB GUSSET: RIGHT WRIST WARMER

Row 1: P1, pm, m1r, pm, p1, work the remaining stitches in the ribbing you knitted earlier.

Rows 2–4: P1, sm, k1, sm, p1, work the remaining stitches in the ribbing you knitted earlier.

Row 5: P1, sm, m1r, k1, m1l, sm, p1, work the remaining stitches in the ribbing you knitted earlier.

Rows 6–8: P1, sm, k to marker, sm, p1, work the remaining stitches in the rib you knitted earlier.

THUMB GUSSET: LEFT WRIST WARMER

Row 1: Work in rib until 1 st remains; pm, m1, pm, p1.

Rows 2–4: Work in rib to the first marker, sm, k1, sm, p1.

Row 5: Work in rib until 1 st remains; sm, m1r, k1, m1l, sm, p1.

Rows 6–8: Work in rib to the first marker, sm, k to next marker, sm, p1.

Repeat Rows 5–8 a further 4 times, and you will now have 11 sts between the markers. Set these aside on a stitch holder or a different coloured piece of yarn and continue to work as per chart and the earlier ribbing.

You will have finished when you reach Row 19 on the second repeat of the chart.

KNIT RIBBING

K2, p2, repeat from * to * to end of row.
Work 4 rows of rib and cast off in rib.

THUMB

Pick up 5 sts around the thumb hole and the 11 sts you set aside previously (16 sts on needles).
Work ribbing: *K2, p2*, repeat from * to * to end of row.
Work 5 rows of rib and cast off in rib.

FINISHING

Fasten off all ends and block the wrist warmers.

CHART 1

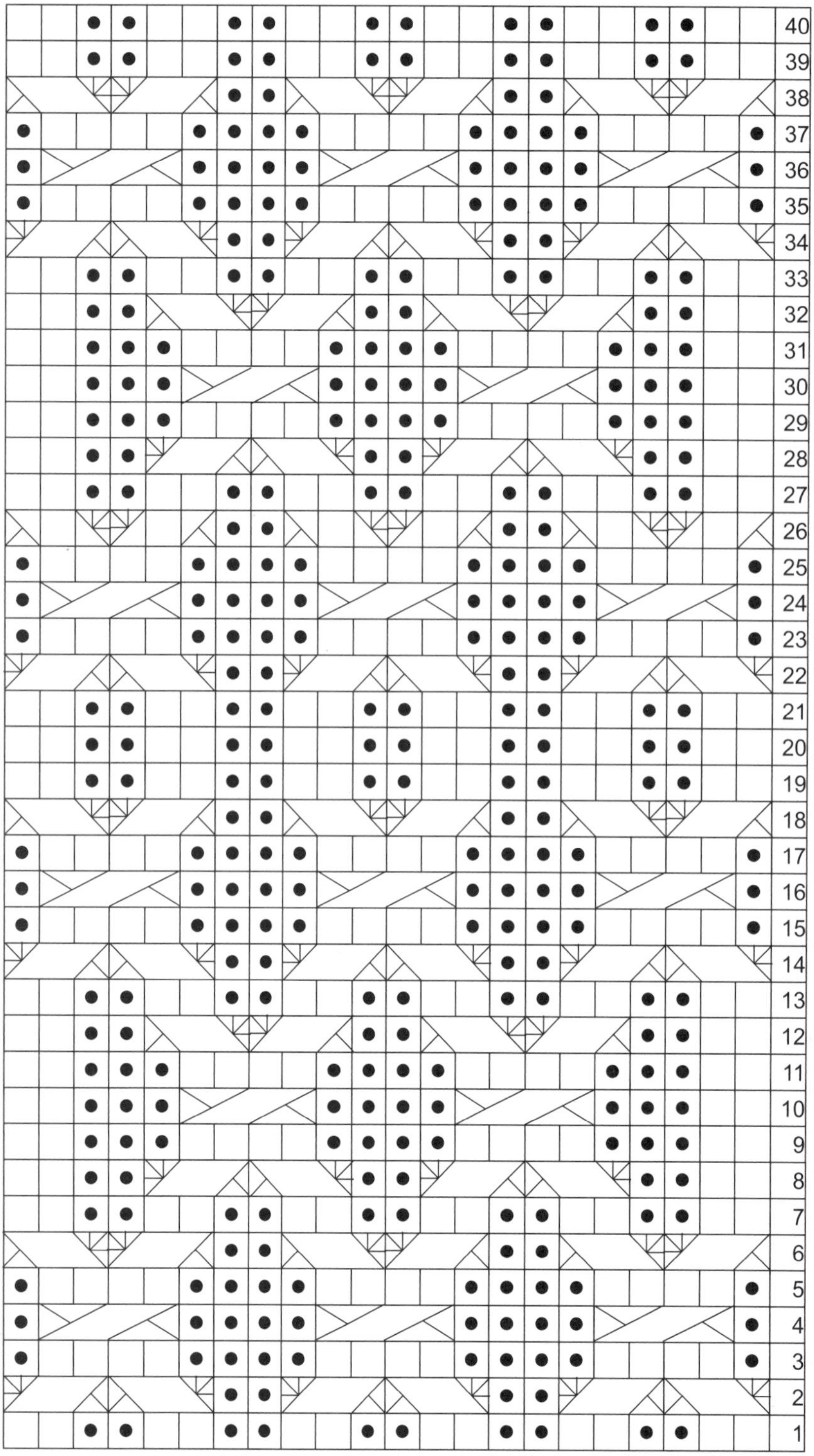
40
39
38
37
36
35
34
33
32
31
30
29
28
27
26
25
24
23
22
21
20
19
18
17
16
15
14
13
12
11
10
9
8
7
6
5
4
3
2
1

 p

 k

Transfer 2 sts to the cable
needle, keep in front of work,
p1, k the sts on the cable needle

Transfer 1 st to the cable needle,
keep behind work, k2, p the st on
the cable needle

Transfer 2 sts to the cable needle,
keep behind work, k2, p the sts on
the cable needle

RACHEL

IVY

Wrist warmers inspired by the 50s and the 70s

INSTRUCTIONS
LEFT WRIST WARMER

Cast on 54 sts in colour A and work 4 rows of ribbing:
K1, p1, repeat from * to * to end of row.
Continue by knitting Row 5 from the bottom of Chart
1 (see page 54), reading left to right. Work up to the
pink marking for the thumb gusset. Now work Chart 2
(see page 55) for the thumb gusset with Chart 1. Place
markers in the pattern so that it is easier to see where
Chart 2 should be.
When you have finished Chart 2 you will have 15 sts
between the markers. Put the 15 sts on a piece of
scrap yarn. Cast on 3 new stitches behind the gusset
and continue to work as per Chart 1.
Cast off in rib.

THUMB

Put the 15 sts from the scrap of yarn back onto the
needles. Pick up another 5 sts in the thumb hole; you
will now have 20 sts on the needles. Work the thumb
as per Chart 3 (see page 55).
Cast off in rib.

RIGHT WRIST WARMER

Work as left wrist warmer, but knit the thumb
gusset on the opposite side of the hand. This is
easiest if you read the row from right to left instead
of from left to right.

FINISHING

Fasten off all ends and block the wrist warmers.

SIZE

Circumference: 18cm (7in) measured
excluding the thumb gusset
Total length: 21.5cm (8½in)
Length of thumb gusset: 6cm (2½in)
*From end of gusset to cast-off of wrist
warmer:* 4cm (1½in)

MATERIALS

Needles: 2.5mm (UK 12, US 2)
Yarn: Rauma Finullgarn
175m/191yds/50g, 100% wool
1 ball in colour A: 423 Brown
1 ball in colour B : 498 Green
1 ball in colour C: 442 Purple

TENSION/GAUGE

30 sts x 36 rows = 10 x 10cm (4 x 4in) in
coloured knitting

CHART 1

CHART 2

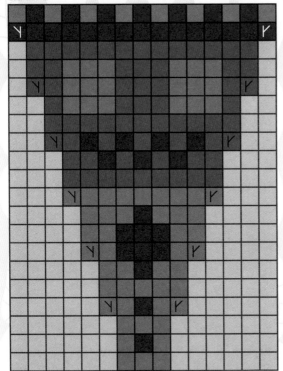

Legend:
- ■ colour A
- ■ colour B
- ■ colour C
- ● p
- Y m1r
- Y m1l
- ■ position of gusset
- ■ no stitch

CHART 3

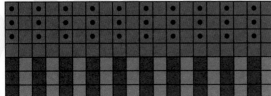

BEAU

Wrist warmers in broken moss stitch

INSTRUCTIONS
LEFT WRIST WARMER
Cast on 56 sts in colour A and work as per Chart 1 (see page 58). Work the chart from the bottom upwards and from right to left. Knit up to the green marking for the gusset.

Now work Chart 2 (see page 59) for the thumb gusset with Chart 1. Place markers in the pattern so that it is easier to see where Chart 2 should be.

When you have finished Chart 2, you will have 17 sts between the markers. Place these 17 sts on a piece of scrap yarn. Cast on 3 new stitches behind the gusset and continue to work as per Chart 1.

Cast off knit on knit and purl on purl.

THUMB
Put the 17 sts from the piece of scrap yarn back on the needles. Pick up another 7 sts in the thumb hole; you will now have 24 sts on the needles. Work the thumb as per Chart 3 (see page 59).

Cast off knit on knit and purl on purl.

RIGHT WRIST WARMER
Work as left wrist warmer, but knit the gusset on the opposite side of the hand. This is easiest if you read the row from left to right.

FINISHING
Fasten off all ends and block the wrist warmers.

SIZE
Circumference: 9.5cm (3¾in) at widest point and 8cm (3¼in) at narrowest
Total length: 18.5cm (7¼in)
Length of thumb gusset: 7cm (2¾in)
From end of gusset to end of wrist warmer: 4.5cm (1¾in)

MATERIALS
Needles: 2.5mm (UK 12, US 2)
Yarn: Sandnes Garn Lanett Babyull 175m/191yds/50g, 100% merino
1 ball colour A = 2317 Yellow
1 ball colour B = 4517 Dark cerise

TENSION/GAUGE
17 sts x 18 rows = 5 x 5cm (2 x 2in) in coloured knitting

CHART 1

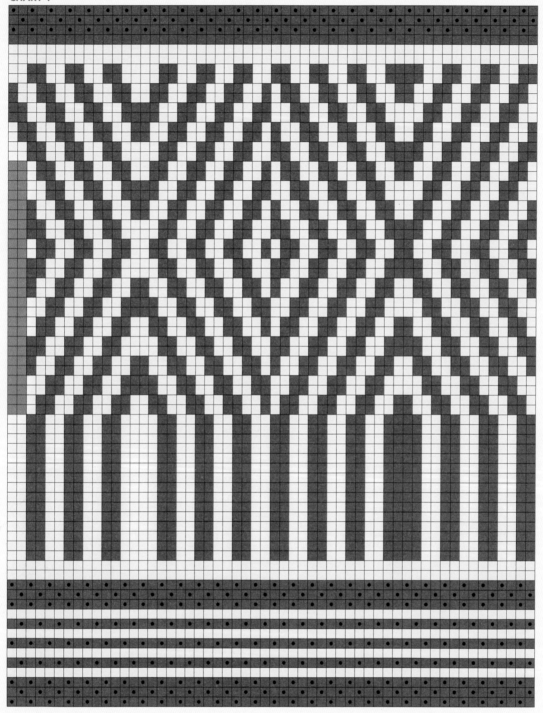

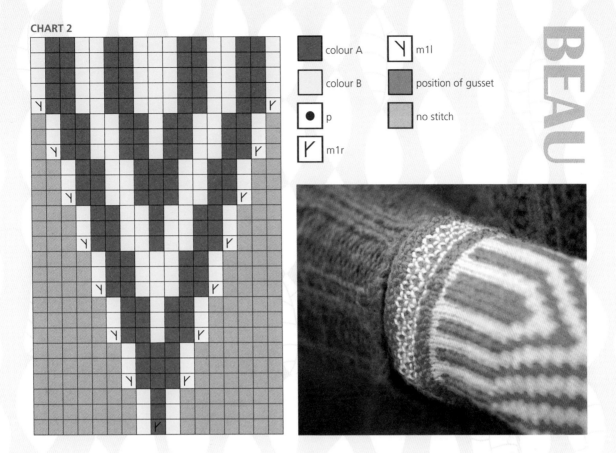

CHART 2

Legend:
- colour A
- colour B
- • p
- Y m1r
- Y m1l
- position of gusset
- no stitch

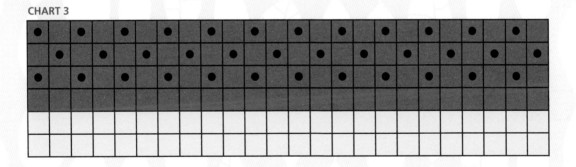

CHART 3

HILDA

Tweed-like wrist warmers in chevron stripes

INSTRUCTIONS
LEFT WRIST WARMER

Cast on 48 sts in colour A and knit 4 rows of ribbing:
K2, p2, repeat from * to * to end of row.
Continue with Row 5 from the bottom of Chart 1
(see page 62), reading left to right. Knit to the green
marking for the thumb gusset. Now work Chart 2
(see page 63) for thumb gusset with Chart 1. Place a
marker in the pattern so that it is easier to see where
Chart 2 should be.
When you have finished Chart 2, you will have 15 sts
between the markers. Place these 15 sts on a piece of
scrap yarn. Cast on 3 new stitches behind the gusset
and continue to work as per Chart 1.
Cast off in rib.

THUMB

Put the 15 sts from the piece of scrap yarn back onto
the needles. Pick up another 5 sts in the thumb hole.
You will now have 20 sts on needles. Work the thumb
as per Chart 3 (see page 63).
Cast off in rib.

RIGHT WRIST WARMER

Work as left wrist warmer, but knit the thumb
gusset on the opposite side of the hand. This is
easiest if you read the row from right to left instead
of from left to right.

FINISHING

Fasten off all ends and block the wrist warmers.

SIZE

Circumference: 17cm (6¾in) excluding the
thumb gusset
Total length: 23cm (9in)
Length of thumb gusset: 7.5cm (3in)
*From end of gusset to cast-off of wrist
warmer:* 4cm (1½in)

MATERIALS

Needles: 3.5mm (UK 9/10, US 4)
Yarn: Rowan Felted Tweed DK
175m/191yds/50g, 50% merino, 25%
viscose, 25% alpaca
1 ball in colour A: 152 Watery
1 ball in colour B: 154 Ginger

TENSION/GAUGE

27 sts x 28 rows = 10 x 10cm (4 x 4in) in
coloured knitting

CHART 1

 colour A

 colour B

⬤ p

Υ m1r

Υ m1l

position of gusset

no stitch

CHART 2

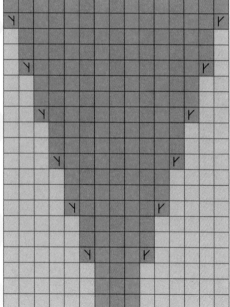

CHART 3

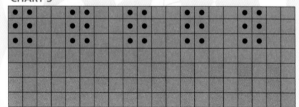

LILY

Embroidered fingerless mitts

SIZE
Circumference: 12cm (4¾in) at widest
point, 9.5cm (3¾in) at narrowest
Total length: 18cm (7in)
Length of thumb gusset: 5.5cm (2¼in)
From end of gusset to end of wrist warmer:
4cm (1½in)

MATERIALS
Needles: 2.5mm (UK 12, US 2)
Yarn: Sandnes Garn Tove
160m/175yds/50g, 100% wool
1 ball in colour A: 7345 Sea green
1 ball in colour B: 6509 Turquoise
1 ball in colour C: 4627 Cerise
1 ball in colour D: 1012 Natural
Plus remnants in various colours
for embroidery

TENSION/GAUGE
17 sts x 17 rows = 5 x 5cm (2 x 2in) in
coloured knitting

INSTRUCTIONS
LEFT MITT
Cast on 52 sts in colour A. Work in moss stitch:
Row 1: *K1, p1*, repeat from * to * to end of row.
Row 2: *P1, k1*, repeat from * to * to end of row.
Row 3: *K1, p1*, repeat from * to * to end of row.
Work one row as follows: *M1, k13*, repeat from
* to * to end of row; you will now have 56 sts.
Now work Chart 1 (see page 66), working from the
bottom up and from right to left. Knit up to the
green marking for the gusset.
Now work Chart 2 (see page 67) for thumb gusset
with Chart 1. Place markers in the pattern so that it
is easier to see where Chart 2 should be.
When you have finished Chart 2 you will have 15
sts between the markers. Place these 15 sts on a
piece of scrap yarn. Cast on 1 new stitch behind
the gusset and continue to work Chart 1.
When you have finished the chart, work a row in
colour A as follows: *Ssk, k12*. You will now have
54 stitches. End with 3 rows of moss stitch as at the
start of the mitt. Cast off purl on knit, knit on purl.

THUMB
Put the 15 sts from the piece of scrap yarn back
on the needles. Pick up another 5 sts in the thumb
hole; you now have 20 sts on the needles. Work
the thumb as per Chart 3 (see page 66), ending
with 3 rows of moss stitch.
Cast off purl on knit, knit on purl.

RIGHT MITT
Work as left mitt, but knit the thumb gusset on
the opposite side of the hand. This is easiest if you
read the row from left to right.

FINISHING
Fasten off all ends and block the mitts. Embroider
a flower on every other square as illustrated, and
work a French knot in the middle of each flower in
yellow yarn (see page 67).

CHART 1

CHART 3

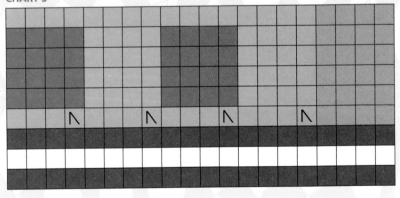

colour A	⅄ m1r
colour B	⅄ m1l
colour C	⅄ ssk
colour D	position of gusset
● p	no stitch

CHART 2

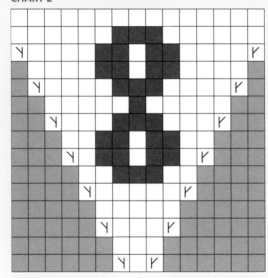

FRENCH KNOT

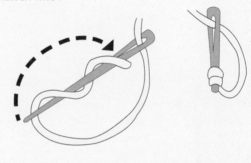

FLOWERS

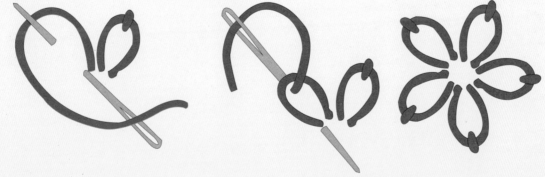

67

KERSTIN

Two-coloured wrist warmers with a 70s feel

INSTRUCTIONS
LEFT WRIST WARMER

Cast on 56 sts in colour A and knit 4 rows of ribbing: *K2, p2*, repeat from * to * to end of row.
Continue by following Row 5 from the bottom of Chart 1 (see page 70), working left to right. Knit up to the green marking for the thumb gusset. Now work Chart 2 (see page 71) for thumb gusset with Chart 1. Place markers in the pattern so that it is easier to see where Chart 2 should be.
When you have finished Chart 2, you will have 15 sts between the markers. Place these 15 sts on a piece of scrap yarn. Cast on 3 new stitches behind the thumb gusset and continue to knit as per Chart 1.
Cast off in rib.

THUMB

Put the 15 sts from the piece of scrap yarn back on the needles. Pick up another 5 sts in the thumb hole; you now have 20 sts on the needles. Work the thumb as per Chart 3 (see page 71).
Cast off in rib.

RIGHT WRIST WARMER

Work as left wrist warmer, but knit the thumb gusset on the opposite side of the hand. This is easiest if you read the row from right to left instead of from left to right.

FINISHING

Fasten off all ends and block the wrist warmers.

SIZE

Circumference: 18cm (7in) measured excluding the thumb gusset
Total length: 26cm (10¼in)
Length of thumb gusset: 7.5cm (3in)
From end of gusset to cast-off of wrist warmer: 5cm (2in)

MATERIALS

Needles: 2.5mm (UK 12, US 2)
Yarn: Kampes 2-ply wool
300m/328yds/100g, 100% wool
1 ball in colour A: 201 Brown
1 ball in colour B: 268 Warm yellow

TENSION/GAUGE

30 sts x 32 rows = 10 x 10cm (4 x 4in) in coloured knitting

CHART 1

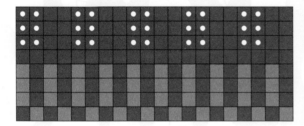

 colour A

colour B

 • p

m1r

 m1l

 position of gusset

no stitch

KERSTIN

CHART 3

CHART 2

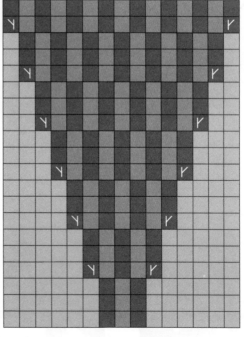

WINTER

ASTRID

Classic winter mittens in three colours with Latvian braid

INSTRUCTIONS
RIGHT MITTEN

Cast on 54 sts in colour A over the thumb and colour B over the forefinger and knit a Latvian braid (see page 12 for instructions). Start working Chart 1 (see page 76), reading it left to right. The horizontal yellow line marks the end of the thumb gusset. When you reach that point, place the 13 sts for the gusset on a piece of scrap yarn.

Cast on 13 sts and continue to knit as per Chart 1. When 8 sts remain, cut off the yarn, leaving a 15cm (6in) tail. Thread the yarn through the remaining stitches and draw up firmly.

THUMB

Put the 13 sts from the piece of scrap yarn back onto the needles. Pick up another 13 sts around thumb hole (13 sts on needles) and work Chart 2 (see page 77). Decrease as for the right mitten.

LEFT MITTEN

Work as right mitten, but swap Rows 2 and 3 of the Latvian braid so that the braid slants in the other direction. Knit the thumb gusset on the opposite side of the hand. This is easiest if you read the row from right to left instead of from left to right.

FINISHING

Fasten off all ends and block the mittens.

SIZE

Circumference: 19cm (7½in)
Length of mitt: 27cm (10¾in)
From thumb to decrease: 14 cm (5½in)
Length of decrease: 4cm (1½in)
Length of thumb: 7cm (2¾in)

MATERIALS

Needles: 2.5mm (UK 12, US 2)
Yarn: Rauma Finullgarn
175m/191yds/50g, 100% wool
1 ball of colour A: 4887 Mint
1 ball of colour B: 401 Off-white
1 ball of colour C: 418 Red

TENSION/GAUGE

32 sts x 32 rows = 10 x 10cm (4 x 4in) in coloured knitting

CHART 1

	colour A
	colour B
	colour C
	position of thumb
⅄	ssk
⅄	k2tog
Ⴘ	m1l
Ⴘ	m1r
	no stitch

CHART 2

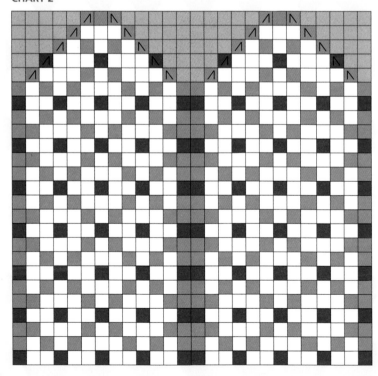

VICKY

Mittens with the now classic wave pattern

INSTRUCTIONS
RIGHT MITTEN
Cast on 56 sts in colour C using an i-cord cast-on (see page 11). Do not break off the yarn, and pick up with colour A. Work Chart 1 (see page 80), reading from left to right. The pink line in the chart marks the position of the thumb. When you reach that point, place 10 sts on a piece of scrap yarn. Cast on 10 sts and continue to work as per Chart 1.
When 8 sts remain, cut off the yarn, leaving a 15cm (6in) tail. Thread the yarn through the remaining stitches and draw up firmly.

THUMB
Pick up the 10 sts you set aside earlier and pick up another 10 sts in the thumb hole (20 sts on needles). Work Chart 2 (see page 81).

LEFT MITTEN
Work as right mitten, but knit the thumb gusset on the opposite side of the hand. This is easiest if you read the row from right to left instead of from left to right.

FINISHING
Sew the i-cord together using Kitchener stitch (see page 14), fasten off all ends and block the mittens.

SIZE
Circumference: 20cm (7¾in)
Length of mitt: 25cm (9¾in)
From thumb to decrease: 7.5 cm (3in)
Length of decrease: 3cm (1¼in)
Length of thumb: 6cm (2½in)

MATERIALS
Needles: 2.5mm (UK 12, US 2)
Yarn: Rauma Finullgarn
175m/191yds/50g, 100% wool
1 ball in colour A: 401 Off-white
1 ball in colour B: 4405 Yellow
1 ball in colour C: 4887 Mint

TENSION/GAUGE
27 sts x 32 rows = 10 x 10cm (4 x 4in) in stocking stitch (US stockinette stitch)

CHART 1

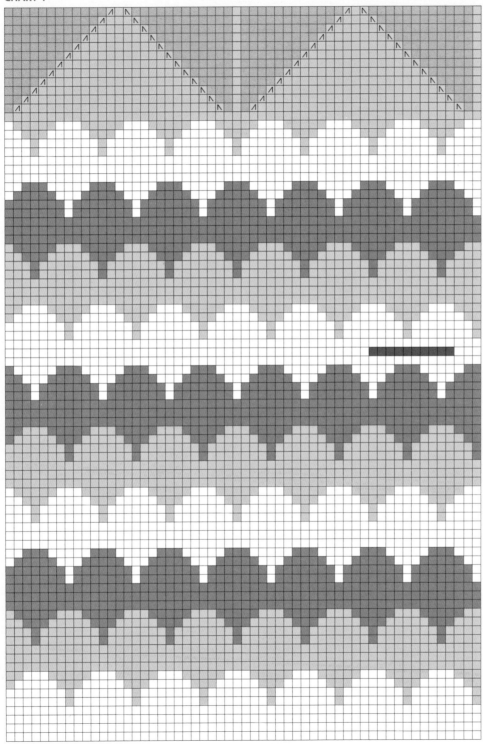

CHART 2

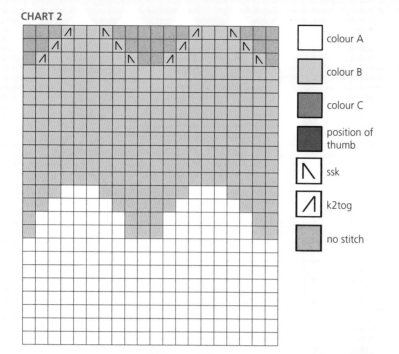

	colour A
	colour B
	colour C
	position of thumb
ssk
k2tog
	no stitch

MARTHA

Practical mittens that are easily turned into wrist warmers

INSTRUCTIONS
LEFT MITTEN

Cast on 56 sts in colour A over the thumb and colour B over the forefinger and knit a Latvian braid (see page 12). Start working Chart 1 (see page 84), reading left to right.

The vertical yellow line marks the thumb gusset and is worked as per Chart 2 (see page 85). When you have finished Chart 2, set aside 13 sts for the gusset on a piece of scrap yarn. Cast on 3 sts and continue to work as per Chart 1. When you have finished the chart, work a Latvian braid. Cast off.

FLIP TOP

You now need to pick up stitches so that you can knit the flip top. These stitches must be picked up in the turquoise row just under the upper section of the pattern – see diagram 1 below.

Using a tapestry needle, insert the end of the yarn at the end of the 28 stitches to be picked up, so that the yarn is on the inside of the mitten. The arrow shows where you need to start picking up stitches; count 28 stitches from that point. The beige stitches in the illustration are where you should pick up the stitches.

DIAGRAM 1

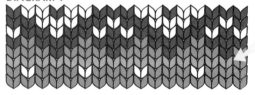

Pick up 28 stitches from the beginning of the row. The last stitch must be picked up next to the inserted end of yarn. Cast on 28 sts using cable cast-on (see page 11), and work as per Chart 3 (see page 85). The first 4 rows should be ribbed, k2, p2, over the 28 cast-on stitches. When you have finished the chart, you will have 4 sts left. K2tog and work an i-cord on the remaining 3 sts for 12 rows. Cast off.

THUMB

Put the 13 sts from the piece of scrap yarn back on the needles and pick up another 11 sts around thumb hole; you now have 24 sts on the needles. Work Chart 4 (see page 85).

RIGHT MITTEN

Work as left mitten, but swap rows 2 and 3 of the Latvian braid so that the braid slants in the other direction. Knit the thumb gusset on the opposite side of the hand. This is easiest if you read the row from right to left instead of from left to right.

FINISHING

Fasten off all ends, sew a button just above the red and white patterned section on the back of each of the hands and block the mittens.

SIZE

Circumference: 18cm (7in) excluding thumb gusset
Length of mitten excluding flip top: 21cm (8¼in)
Length of thumb: 6.5 cm (2½in)
Length of flip top: 10cm (4in)

MATERIALS

Needles: 2.5mm (UK 12, US 2)
Yarn: Rauma Finullgarn

175m/191yds/50g, 100% wool
1 ball in colour A: 4705 Turquoise
1 ball in colour B: 401 Off-white
1 ball in colour C: 418 Red

BUTTONS

2, approx. 15mm (in) in diameter.

TENSION/GAUGE

30 sts x 33 rows = 10 x 10cm (4 x 4in) in stocking stitch (US stockinette stitch)

CHART 1

CHART 2

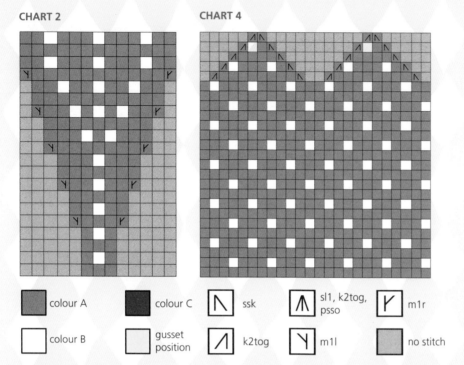

CHART 4

| | colour A | | colour C | 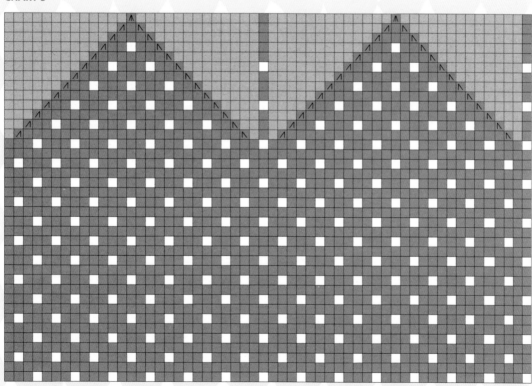 ↖ | ssk | ↟ | sl1, k2tog, psso | ⅄ | m1r |
| | colour B | | gusset position | ↗ | k2tog | Ⅎ | m1l | | no stitch |

CHART 3

DORIS

You can never have too many dots and buttons!

INSTRUCTIONS
LEFT MITTEN
Cast on 54 sts in colour A using an i-cord cast-on (see page 11). Do not break off the yarn, and pick up with colour A.
Work Chart 1 (see page 88), reading left to right. The horizontal red line in the chart marks the end of the thumb gusset. When you reach that point, place 13 sts on a piece of scrap yarn. Cast on 13 sts and continue to work Chart 1. When you have 8 sts left, cut the yarn, leaving a 15cm (6in) tail. Thread the yarn through the remaining stitches and draw up firmly.

THUMB
Put the 13 sts from the piece of scrap yarn back onto the needles. Pick up another 13 sts around the thumb hole (26 sts on needles). Work Chart 2 (see page 89).

RIGHT MITTEN
Work as left mitten, but knit the thumb gusset on the opposite side of the hand. This is easiest if you read the row from right to left instead of from left to right.

FINISHING
Sew the i-cord together with Kitchener stitch (see page 14), fasten off all ends and block the mittens.

SIZE
Circumference: 18cm (7in), measured above the thumb gusset
Total length: 24cm (9½in)
Length of thumb gusset: 5.5cm (2¼in)
From end of thumb gusset to end of mitten: 13.5cm (5¼in)

MATERIALS
Needles: 2.5mm (UK 12, US 2)
Yarn: Rauma Finullgarn
175m/191yds/50g, 100% wool
1 ball in colour A: 455 Green
1 ball in colour B: 4405 Yellow

TENSION/GAUGE
32 sts x 36 rows = 10 x 10cm (4 x 4in) in coloured knitting

CHART 1

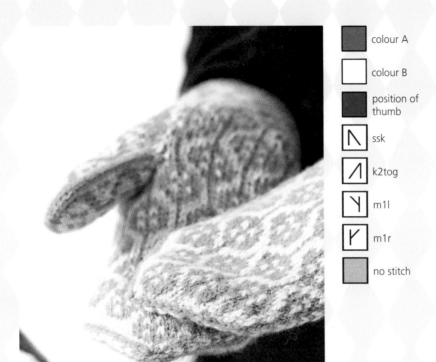

	colour A
	colour B
	position of thumb
 ssk
k2tog
m1l
m1r
	no stitch

DORIS

CHART 2

BETHAN

Mittens for newlyweds

INSTRUCTIONS
LEFT MITTEN
Cast on 60 sts in colour A.
Knit twisted ribbing: *K1tbl, p1*, repeat from * to *
to end of row for 5 rows. Then knit a Latvian braid (see
page 12 for instructions). Start working Chart 1 (see
page 92), reading left to right. For the yellow section
of the chart, use either Chart 3, 4 or 5 (see page 93),
depending on which couple you want.
The horizontal blue line marks the end of the thumb
gusset. When you reach that point, set the 13 sts for
the gusset aside on a piece of scrap yarn. Cast on 13
sts and continue to knit Chart 1.
When you have 12 sts left, cut the yarn, leaving a
15cm (6in) tail. Thread the yarn through the remaining
stitches and draw up firmly.

THUMB
Put the 13 sts from the piece of scrap yarn back on the
needles. Pick up another 13 sts around the thumb hole
(26 sts on needles) and work Chart 2 (see page 93).
Finish off as for the mitten.

RIGHT MITTEN
Work as left mitten, but swap Rows 2 and 3 of the
Latvian braid so that the braid slants in the other
direction. Knit the thumb gusset on the opposite side
of the hand. This is easiest if you read the row from
right to left instead of from left to right.

FINISHING
Fasten off all ends and block the mittens.

SIZE
Circumference: 21cm (8¼in)
Length of mitten: 26cm (10¼in)
From thumb to decrease: 9cm (3½in)
Length of decrease: 4cm (1½in)

MATERIALS
Needles: 2.5mm (UK 12, US 2)
Yarn: Sandnes Garn Sisu
160m/175yds/50g, 80% wool, 20% nylon
1 ball in colour A: 4219 Red
2 balls in colour B: 1012 Natural
2 balls in colour C: 1088 Coke
Amount of yarn given is for two pairs
of mittens

TENSION/GAUGE
32 sts x 32 rows = 10 x 10cm (4 x 4in) in
coloured knitting

CHART 1

CHART 3

◼ (dark red)	colour A
☐ (white)	colour B
◼ (black)	colour C
◼ (grey)	position of thumb
☐ (light)	position of charts 3–5

⟍	ssk
⟋	k2tog
⅄	m1l
Ⅴ	m1r
◼ (light grey)	no stitch

CHART 4

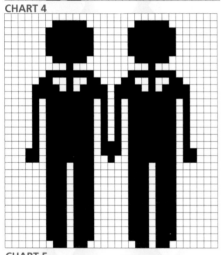

CHART 5

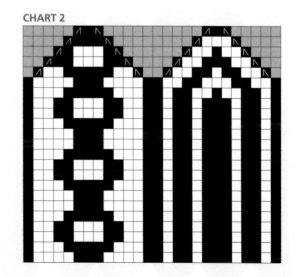

CHART 2

ESTHER

With playful cats and balls of wool

INSTRUCTIONS
RIGHT MITTEN

Cast on 56 sts in colour A, and knit ribbing: *K2, p2*, repeat from * to * to end for 17 rows. Then start Chart 1 (see page 96), reading left to right.

The horizontal yellow line marks the end of the thumb gusset. When you reach that point, put aside the 13 sts for the gusset on a piece of scrap yarn. Cast on 13 sts and continue to work Chart 1.

When you have 10 sts left, cut off the yarn, leaving a 15cm (6in) tail. Thread the yarn through the remaining stitches and draw up firmly.

THUMB

Put the 13 sts from the piece of scrap yarn back on the needles. Pick up another 13 sts around thumb hole (26 sts on needles) and work Chart 2 (see page 97). Decrease as for the right mitten.

LEFT MITTEN

Work as right mitten, but knit the thumb gusset on the opposite side of the hand. This is easiest if you read the row from right to left instead of from left to right.

FINISHING

Fasten off all ends and block the mittens.

SIZE

Circumference: 20cm (7¾in)
Length of mitten: 25cm (9¾in)
From thumb to decrease: 9cm (3½in)
Length of thumb: 7cm (2¾in)

MATERIALS

Needles: 2.5mm (UK 12, US 2)
Yarn: Rauma Finullgarn
175m/191yds/50g, 100% wool
1 ball in colour A: 4605 Dark blue
1 ball in colour B: 4705 Light blue

TENSION/GAUGE

30 sts x 32 rows = 10 x 10cm (4 x 4in) in coloured knitting

CHART 1

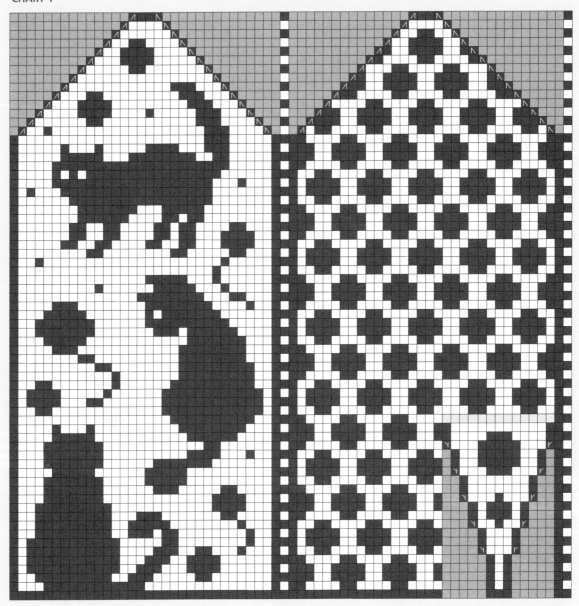

CHART 2

- ⬛ colour A
- ⬜ colour B
- 🟫 position of thumb
- ⟍ ssk
- ⟋ k2tog
- ⅄ m1l
- Ⅎ m1r
- ⬛ no stitch

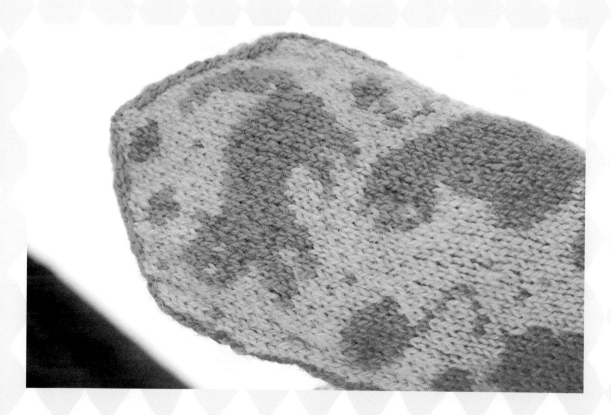

SACHA

Classic mittens in red, white and blue

INSTRUCTIONS
RIGHT MITTEN

Cast on 54 sts in colour B over the thumb and colour C over the forefinger, and knit a Latvian braid (see page 12 for instructions). Continue working Chart 1 (see page 100), working left to right.

When you reach the horizontal yellow line, place the 13 sts for the thumb gusset on a piece of scrap yarn. Cast on 13 sts and continue to work the chart. When you have 8 sts left, cut off the yarn, leaving a 15cm (6in) tail. Thread the yarn through the remaining stitches and draw up firmly.

THUMB

Put the 13 sts from the piece of scrap yarn back onto the needles. Pick up another 13 sts around thumb hole (26 sts on needles) and work Chart 2 (see page 101). Decrease as for the right mitten.

LEFT MITTEN

Work as right mitten, but swap Rows 2 and 3 of the Latvian braid so that the braid slants in the other direction. Knit the thumb gusset on the opposite side of the hand. This is easiest if you read the row from right to left instead of from left to right.

FINISHING

Fasten off all ends and block the mittens.

SIZE

Circumference: 21cm (8¼in)
Length of mitten: 25cm (9¾in)
From thumb to decrease: 11cm (4¼in)
Length of decrease: 4cm (1½in)
Length of thumb: 7cm (2¾in)

MATERIALS

Needles: 2.5mm (UK 12, US 2)
Yarn: Debbie Bliss Baby Cashmerino 125m/136yds/50g, 55% merino wool, 33% acrylic, 12% cashmere
1 ball colour A: 204 Baby blue
1 ball in colour B: 101 Ecru
1 ball in colour C: 034 Red

TENSION/GAUGE

30 sts x 32 rows = 10 x 10cm (4 x 4in) in coloured knitting

CHART 1

CHART 2

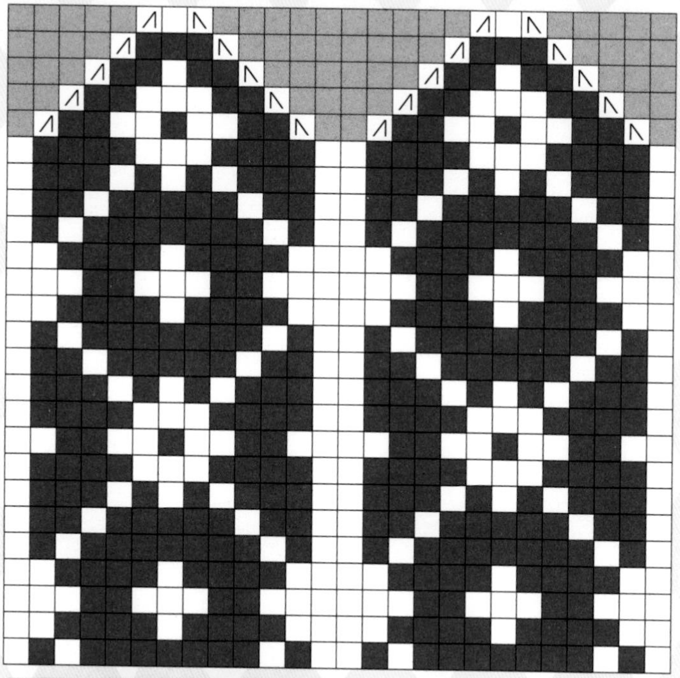

SACHA

Legend:

- colour A
- colour B
- colour C
- position of thumb
- ssk
- k2tog
- m1l
- m1r
- no stitch

SIAN
Stylised birds and Latvian braid

INSTRUCTIONS
RIGHT MITTEN
Cast on 56 sts in colour A over the thumb and colour C over the forefinger, and knit a Latvian braid (see page 12 for instructions). Start working Chart 1 (see page 104), reading left to right. The horizontal blue line marks the end of the thumb gusset. When you reach that point, place the 13 sts for the gusset on a piece of scrap yarn. Cast on 13 sts and continue to work Chart 1.
When you have 10 sts left, cut off the yarn, leaving a 15cm (6in) tail. Thread the yarn through the remaining stitches and draw up firmly.

THUMB
Put the 13 sts from the piece of scrap yarn back on the needles. Pick up another 13 sts around thumb hole (26 sts on needles) and work Chart 2 (see page 105).

LEFT MITTEN
Knit as right mitten, but swap Rows 2 and 3 of the Latvian braid so that the braid slants in the other direction. Knit the thumb gusset on the opposite side of the hand. This is easiest if you read the row from right to left instead of from left to right.

FINISHING
Fasten off all ends and block the mittens.

SIZE
Circumference: 19cm (7½in)
Length of mitten: 27cm (10¾in)
From thumb to decrease: 14cm (5½in)
Length of decrease: 4cm (1½in)
Length of thumb: 7cm (2¾in)

MATERIALS
Needles: 2.5mm (UK 12, US 2)
Yarn: Kampes 2-ply wool
300m/328yds/100g, 100% wool
1 skein in colour A: 201 Brown
1 skein in colour B: 268 Warm yellow
1 skein in colour C: White

TENSION/GAUGE
32 sts x 32 rows = 10 x 10cm (4 x 4in) in coloured knitting

CHART 1

CHART 2

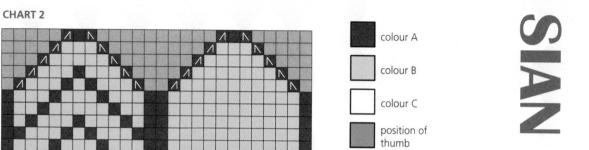

- ■ colour A
- ▨ colour B
- □ colour C
- ▨ position of thumb
- ⋀ ssk
- ⋀ k2tog
- ⅄ m1l
- Ⅎ m1r
- ▨ no stitch

SAM
Classic star mittens

INSTRUCTIONS
LEFT MITTEN
Cast on 54 sts in colour B using an i-cord cast-on (see page 11). Do not break the yarn. Pick up with colour A. Work Chart 1 (see page 108), reading left to right. The horizontal yellow line in the chart marks the end of the thumb gusset. When you reach that point, place 13 sts on a piece of scrap yarn. Cast on 13 sts and continue to work Chart 1.
When you have 8 sts left, cut off the yarn, leaving a 15cm (6in) tail. Thread the yarn through the remaining stitches and draw up firmly.

THUMB
Put the 13 sts from the piece of scrap yarn back on the needles. Pick up another 13 sts around thumb hole (26 sts on needles). Work Chart 2 (see page 109).

RIGHT MITTEN
Knit as left mitten, but knit the thumb gusset on the opposite side of the hand. This is easiest if you read the row from right to left instead of from left to right.

FINISHING
Fasten off all ends. Sew the i-cord together using Kitchener stitch (see page 14).

SIZE
Circumference: 20cm (7¾in), measured above the thumb gusset
Total length: 22cm (8¾in)
Length of thumb gusset: 4.5cm (1¾in)
From end of thumb gusset to end of mitten: 13.5cm (5¼in)

MATERIALS
Needles: 2.5mm (UK 12, US 2)
Yarn: Sandnes Garn Tove
160m/175yds/50g, 100% wool
1 ball in colour A: 1053 Mixed grey
1 ball in colour B: 2206 Yellow

TENSION/GAUGE
32 sts x 32 rows = 10 x 10cm (4 x 4in) in coloured knitting

CHART 1

CHART 2

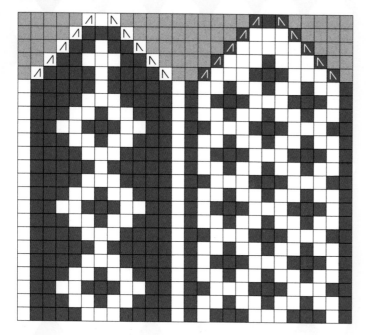

 colour A   ⋀ k2tog

□ colour B   Y m1l

▢ position of thumb   Y m1r

⋀ ssk   ▢ no stitch

SAM

SIZE
Circumference: 19cm (7½in)
Length of mitten: 25cm (9¾in)
From thumb to decrease: 9cm (3½in)
Length of decrease: 4cm (1½in)
Length of thumb: 7cm (2¾in)

MATERIALS
Needles: 4mm (UK 8, US 6)
Yarn: Drops Nepal
75m/82yds/50g, 65% wool, 35% alpaca
2 skeins in colour A: 0612 Medium brown
1 skein in colour B: 0100 Off-white

TENSION/GAUGE
18 sts x 27 rows = 10 x 10cm (4 x 4in) in
stocking stitch (US stockinette stitch)

FRANCIS

Simple mittens with a patterned border

INSTRUCTIONS

Cast on 32 sts in colour A. Knit ribbing: *K1, p1*, repeat from * to * for 5 rows. K one row, then work Chart 1 (see below); repeat the chart around the whole mitten. Break off colour B and continue to knit the rest of the mitten in colour A. Knit 5 rows, then work the thumb gusset.

THUMB GUSSET: RIGHT MITTEN

Row 1: K1, pm, m1r, pm, k to end of row.
Rows 2–3: K1, sm, k1, sm, k to end of row.
Row 4: K1, sm, m1r, k to next marker, m1l, sm, K to end of row.
Rows 5–6: K1, sm, k to marker, sm, k to end of row.

THUMB GUSSET: LEFT MITTEN

Row 1: K until 1 st remaining, pm, m1, pm, k1.
Rows 2–3: K to first marker, sm, k1, sm, k1.
Row 4: K to first marker, sm, m1r, k to next marker, m1l, sm, k1.
Rows 5–6: K to first marker, sm, k to next marker, sm, k1.
Repeat Rows 4–6 another 5 times. You will now have 13 stitches between the markers. Set these stitches aside on a stitch holder or a different coloured piece of yarn and continue to knit until the mitten is about 4cm (1½in) shorter than its final size.
Now, decrease as follows:
Row 1: On needles 1 and 3: Ssk, k remaining stitches.
On needles 2 and 4: K until 2 sts remain, k2tog.
Row 2: K.

Repeat these two rows until 8 sts remain. Cut off the yarn, leaving a 15cm (6in) tail. Thread the yarn through the remaining stitches and draw up firmly.

THUMB

Put the 13 sts you set aside earlier back on the needles. Pick up another 3 sts around thumb hole (16 sts on needles). K round until about 1cm (½in) shorter than its final size.
Decrease as follows:
On needles 1 and 3: Ssk, k remaining stitches.
On needles 2 and 4: K until 2 stitches remain, k2tog.
Repeat this row twice. Cut off the yarn, thread it through the remaining stitches and draw up firmly.

FINISHING

Fasten off all ends and block the mittens.

CHART 1

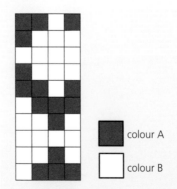

colour A

colour B

OTTO

Mittens with print motif and colour detail

INSTRUCTIONS

LEFT MITTEN

Cast on 54 sts in colour A over the thumb and colour B over the forefinger, and knit a Latvian braid (see page 12 for instructions). Start working Chart 1 (see page 114), reading from left to right. The horizontal red line marks the end of the thumb gusset. When you reach that point, set aside the 13 sts for the gusset on a piece of scrap yarn. Cast on 13 sts and continue to work Chart 1.

You will now have 8 sts. Cut off the yarn, leaving a 15cm (6in) tail. Thread the yarn through the remaining stitches and draw up firmly.

THUMB

Put the 13 sts from the piece of scrap yarn back on the needles. Pick up another 13 sts around thumb hole (26 sts on needles) and work Chart 2 (see page 115). Finish off as for the mitten.

RIGHT MITTEN

Work as left mitten, but swap Rows 2 and 3 of the Latvian braid so that the braid slants in the other direction. Knit the thumb gusset on the opposite side of the hand. This is easiest if you read the row from right to left instead of from left to right.

FINISHING

Fasten off all ends and block the mittens.

SIZE

Circumference: 20cm (7¾in)
Length of mitten: 25cm (9¾in)
From thumb to decrease: 11cm (4¼in)
Length of decrease: 3.5cm (1½in)
Length of thumb: 7cm (2¾in)

MATERIALS

Needles: 2.5mm (UK 12, US 2)
Yarn: Sandnes Garn Tove
160m/175yds/50g, 100% wool
1 ball in colour A: 1012 Natural
1 ball in colour B: 1088 Coke
1 ball in colour C: 6509 Turquoise

TENSION/GAUGE

32 sts x 32 rows = 10 x 10cm (4 x 4in) in coloured knitting

CHART 1

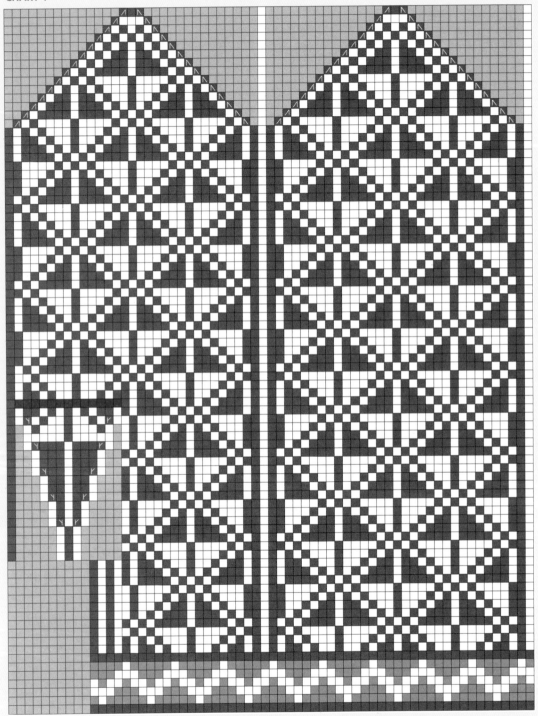

CHART 2

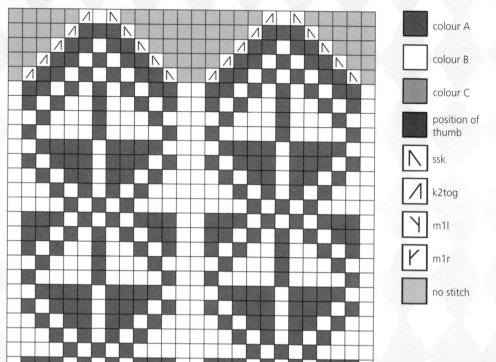

■	colour A
□	colour B
■	colour C
■	position of thumb
⋀	ssk
⋀	k2tog
⋎	m1l
⋎	m1r
■	no stitch

TALULA
Mittens inspired by peacocks

INSTRUCTIONS
LEFT MITTEN
Cast on 54 sts in colour C using an i-cord cast-on (see page 11). Break off the yarn and pick up with colour A.
Work Chart 1 (see page 118), reading left to right. The horizontal yellow line in the chart marks the end of the thumb gusset. When you reach that point, place 13 sts on a piece of scrap yarn. Cast on 13 sts and continue to work Chart 1. When there are 8 sts remaining, cut off the yarn, leaving a 15cm (6in) tail. Thread the yarn through the remaining stitches and draw up firmly.

THUMB
Put the 13 sts from the piece of scrap yarn back onto the needles. Pick up another 13 sts around thumb hole (26 sts on needles). Work Chart 2 (see page 119).

RIGHT MITTEN
Work as left mitten, but knit the thumb gusset on the opposite side of the hand. This is easiest if you read the row from right to left instead of from left to right.

FINISHING
Sew the i-cord together using Kitchener stitch (see page 14), fasten off all ends and block the mittens.

SIZE
Circumference: 19cm (7¾in), measured above the thumb gusset
Total length: 25cm (9¾in)
Length of thumb gusset: 5cm (4¼in)
From end of thumb gusset to end of mitten: 13.5cm (2¾in)

MATERIALS
Needles: 2.5mm (UK 12, US 2)
Yarn: Sandnes Garn Tove
160m/175yds/50g, 100% wool
1 ball in colour A: 2641 Natural
Scraps in colour C: 1099 Black
Kauni 2-ply
350m/382yds/100g, 100% wool
1 ball in colour B: RR Grass green

TENSION/GAUGE
32 sts x 32 rows = 10 x 10cm (4 x 4in) in coloured knitting

CHART 1

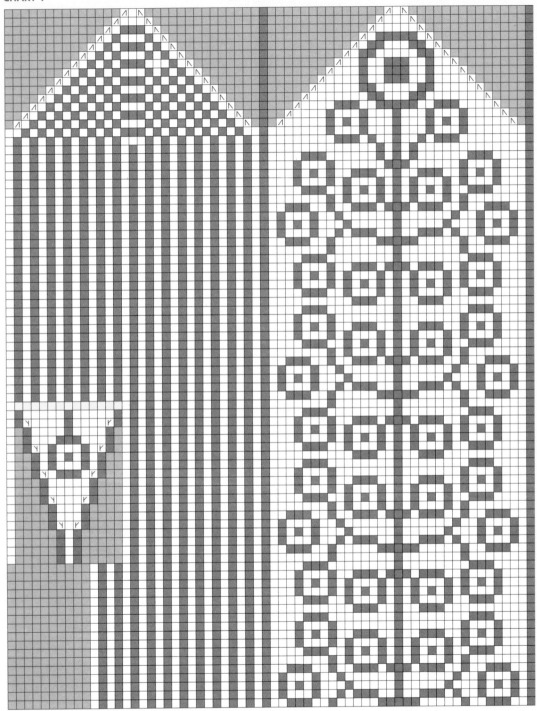

	colour A
	colour B
	position of thumb
⟋	ssk
⟋	k2tog
Ⅴ	m1l
Ⅴ	m1r
	no stitch

CHART 2

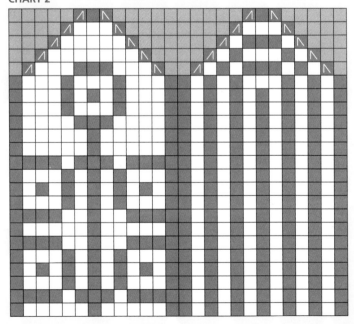

JAMTLI

One of the most popular tourist destinations in Östersund (in central Sweden), Jamtli is a museum whose attractive buildings and grounds house important collections of archaeological objects and textiles.

It has a programme of indoor and outdoor activities including festivals, exhibitions, markets and historical walks. Storytellers are on site to tell visitors what existence was like in previous times, regarding both everyday life and special occasions. To find out more, visit www.jamtli.com.

We photographed the winter chapter of the book in the beautiful surroundings of the museum; many thanks to the staff at Jamtli for making us welcome during those snowy days.

THANK YOU

To Andreas and Henrik for their support.

To Elin D, Inger, Emma, Eva-Karin, Elin T, Karin, Silje, Anna, Josefine, Malin, Stina, Catarina and Johanna for their help testing the patterns.

To Anna, Sanna, Nina and Henrik for acting as models for our photographs.

YOUR NOTES